Happy 11th
Love, Am..

Meet the Police Dogs

The K-9 Cops

Meet the Police Dogs
By Christy Judah

ISBN   978-1-4495-5265-7
144-955265X

C. Joyce C. Judah, 2009, All Rights Reserved.
Published by Coastal Books.

Original Front Cover Art Portrait by Laurie Gayle;
www.lauriegayle.com
Raleigh, NC. Front cover: K-9 Axe of the Raleigh Police Department, Raleigh, NC.

At Left: K-9's Otto & Rudy, Raleigh Police Department, Raleigh, NC. Portrait by L. Gayle.

Back Cover Photograph of K-9 Arko. Wilmington Police Department, Wilmington, NC

Other books by Christy Judah include:
The Two Faces of Dixie: Politicians, Plantations and Slaves   978-1442134843
The Legends of Brunswick County: Ghosts, Pirates, Indians and Colonial North Carolina   978-0615175867
An Ancient History of Dogs: Spaniels Through the Ages 978-143031861
The Faircloth Family History   978-0788444722
The Faircloth Family Genealogy: Edward Farecloth Lineage   978-1442104396
The Faircloth Family Genealogy: William Faircloth I Lineage 978-1442101050
The Faircloth Family Genealogy Resources 978-1441495112
The Best of the Beaches: Brunswick County ASIN: B0029J4K6U
Building a Basic Foundation for Search and Rescue Dog Training   978-1430328056
Buzzards and Butterflies: Human Remains Detection Dogs 978-0615202280
Meet the Search and Rescue Dogs   978-1448684939

Contact information:
christyjudah@christyjudah.com ; (910) 842-7942;
Web Links: www.christyjudah.com
All books available on Amazon.com

Coastal Books

Printed in the United States of America.

Dedication

*To All Police Dogs and their handlers,
present, past, and future,
especially those who gave their all.
Thank you from the bottom of our hearts.*

*Right: K-9 Tjibbe, DeKalb County School Police Department, GA.
Left: K-9 Clyde, Bloodhound Puppy, Brunswick County Sheriff Department, NC*

MEET THE POLICE DOGS

The K-9 Cops

Art by Laurie Gayle

Top: K-9's Bene and Beny   Bottom: K-9 Beny - Sampson County Sheriff Department, NC

My name is *K-9 Bene* and

I am a police dog .... a K-9 cop that is.

I am just one of many police dogs working all over the world.

Let me introduce you to some of my friends.

We work many types of law enforcement jobs with our partners.

K-9 Bene, Sampson County Sheriff Department
Sampson County, NC

We work for many different organizations such as Police and Sheriff Departments, state and federal agencies, and airports. We even work for specialized departments like Homeland Security, the State Bureau of Investigation, and the Federal Bureau of Investigation.

But no matter whom we work for, we work to protect and serve all citizens.

K-9 Ranger, Edmonds Police Department, Edmonds, Washington

K-9 Axel, NHSD
New Hanover County, NC

K9 Behr, Raleigh PD
Raleigh, NC

K-9 Aron, NHSD
New Hanover County, NC

K-9 Bonnie, Bloodhound Puppy, BCSD
Brunswick County, NC

K-9 Beny, SCSD
Sampson County, NC

Above: K-9 Deon, Wilmington Police Department, Wilmington, NC

Right: K-9 Beny, Sampson County Sheriff Department, Sampson County, NC

We attend Police Dog School and receive special training to become a certified K-9 Cop. Only the best are chosen for this job…. the smartest, most loyal and those dogs willing to be trained and worked. During Police Dog School, we learn all kinds of obedience skills such as *sit, stay, come, climb, jump, wait, crawl,* and *down*.

Learning to *climb* and *jump* over obstacles takes practice and discipline. It has to be perfect!

New Hanover County Sheriff Department, Wilmington, NC

Above: K-9 Axe   Left: K-9 Jago
Raleigh Police Department, Raleigh, NC

**We learn to leap over boxes and
will check to see
if there is a person hiding inside.**

*New Hanover County Sheriff Department Training Grounds
New Hanover County, NC*

My friend, ARCO, jumps the hurdles and the broad jump for the Wilmington Police Department in Wilmington, NC.

After many sessions of practice and training, the dogs and handlers are certified and graduate from Police Dog School. Only the finest become police dogs.

Ofc. K. Vithalani and K-9 Arco, Wilmington PD, Wilmington, NC

K-9 Bronco, Wilmington PD, Wilmington, NC

K-9 Bronco gives his handler, Officer Stansbury, a big graduation kiss and hug!!

Police Dogs sometimes work at airports where they may sniff suitcases and luggage. Beagles are often used for this important job because of their friendly nature and appearance. Some beagles that work for the United States Department of Homeland Security are called the "*Beagle Brigade.*"

K-9 Arko, Wilmington PD, Wilmington, NC

And sometimes the dogs compete with other police dogs to see who is quickest, most agile, or best in performing a certain skill. K-9 Cyndi shows off her trophy wins for the Wilmington PD.

The dog's sense of smell is almost 50 times better than a human nose. They can sniff out all kinds of things including fruit, narcotics, weapons, or bombs.

K-9 Bruno, Wilmington PD
Right: K-9 Taz & Officer T. Bell of DeKalb County School Police Depart. GA

A Brief History of Police Dogs

Dogs have been used to assist humans as guard dogs throughout all time. Even in early Roman and Greek cities, long before many breeds were formally named, the early dogs, such as Mossolians (the precursors to the mastiff and ancestors of the bloodhounds), were *working dogs that were used to protect and hunt*.

Officially, Police Departments in Europe were using bloodhounds as early as the 1700s but it wasn't until the early 1900s that countries such as Germany and Belgium began formally training dogs for police work. They were first used as guard dogs. Soon after that, dog-training programs were established all across Europe. The United States became involved in widely training police dogs by the 1960s. About that time they were recognized as a vital part of law enforcement.

Currently, many departments employ police dogs to assist the officers with their duties. Dogs have served in active service at the sides of their handlers and owners, and have often been the hero showing great bravery under fire, saving lives (often by sacrificing their own), and bringing comfort to the injured, especially during a time of war. They continue to serve today.

Police dogs learn to sniff out many types of smells including the odor of people. This is called "trailing" or "tracking" depending upon the type of training.

Many trailing dogs work with a long rope or "lead" attached to their harness. Putting on the harness tells the dog that he is going to work.

Top: K-9 Luka, Handler: S. L. Lowery, Raleigh Police Department, Raleigh, NC

Bottom: K-9 Chenok, Handler: C. T. Barnett, Raleigh Police Department, Raleigh, NC

Bloodhounds, like K-9 Duke, are often used as trailing dogs. These dogs can follow the path where a person has walked or run. This helps the officer to find missing people or catch a criminal who has run from the police.

A trailing dog might locate a robber who has tried to steal something that didn't belong to him. Or he may look for a little boy or girl who has wondered away from home and gotten lost.

so cool!

> Remember:
> Never leave home alone...
> take along a buddy.

K-9 Duke, Bloodhound, at four-years old, Sampson County Sheriff Department, Sampson County, NC.

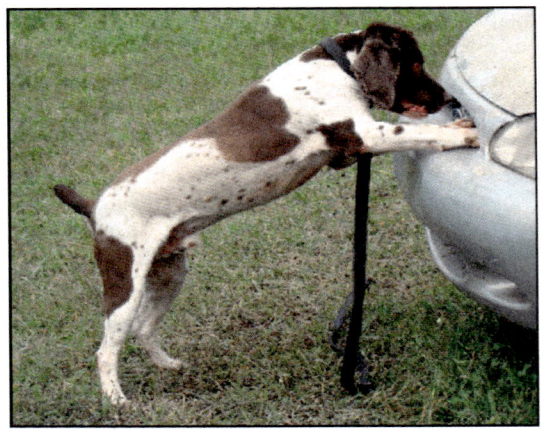

K-9 Rocky, DeKalb School PD
DeKalb County, GA

K-9 Beny, Sampson County SD
Sampson County, NC

Above: K-9 Chris, Snellville PD, GA
Left: Ofc. J. Brooks, K-9 Rocky,
DeKalb County, NC

Some police dogs are trained to search vehicles….
They look on the inside and the outside…. around the wheels
or in the trunk…anywhere a person might hide drugs.

Bomb dogs are trained to find explosives or bombs. These dogs have a very special job. They help keep the soldiers, marines, and airmen safe around the world. They can sniff out a bomb no matter where it is hidden. Bomb dogs train every week to keep their skills sharp.

Handler Jess Hunter and K-9 Zhirra Bomb Dog Who Worked in Iraq in late 2005.

These dogs can find explosives located in cars, buildings, boxes and airplanes.
They can sniff anywhere looking for explosive materials.

K-9 Arco, Wilmington PD, Wilmington, NC

K-9 Behr, Raleigh Police Department, Raleigh, NC

Police dogs are here to assist and support our uniformed officer as he or she responds to burglar alarms, robberies, fleeing suspects, or searches for illegal or stolen goods.

They do area searches, building searches, evidence searches, and tracking problems.

It takes a "special person "to become a police dog handler. The handler is carefully selected, must be in good physical shape to keep pace with the dog. They must be willing to have a canine as their law enforcement partner and enjoy working with dogs.

Handler Tracy Sargent and K-9 Cinco, from Georgia

Sometimes the police dog will visit with school children. The dog handler will talk about the job duties and a typical day in the life of a law enforcement dog.

The dog might demonstrate his police dog skills and allow others to pet him. The students are always encouraged to be good citizens and stay away from drugs.

Remember:

*Stay away from drugs, and obey the law at all times.
And always ask permission before approaching another dog.*

K-9 Gola, Raleigh Police Department, Raleigh, NC

Law Enforcement dogs can help keep us safe. Here I am with my partner, Cpl. Scott Grantham. Together we found 251 pounds of marijuana, a proud moment for both of us.

Lots of drugs were taken off the street that day.

K-9 Bene, Dep. D. Carter; Sampson County Sheriff Department, Sampson County, NC

K-9 Beny, Dep. S. Grantham and D. Carter.
Sampson County Sheriff Department, Sampson County, NC

**And here is my friend, K-9 Beny.
He found over $140,000 in stolen cash.
Good job Beny.**

K-9 Benny

K-9 Bruno
Brunswick County Sheriff Dept., Brunswick County, NC

K-9 Spike

Many departments have several working police dogs. Some have specialties and others work as general patrol dogs who look for fleeing felons......criminals who try to run from the police.

And some police dogs work at prisons, specifically trained to find persons who have escaped from the prison. These dogs are called "prison dogs."

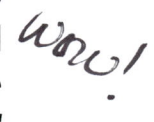

wow!

K-9 Rex, Dep. D. Carter SCSD, Sampson County, NC

**Remember: Stealing is Wrong....and against the law.
Never, ever steal anything.**

Some dogs have a specialty in Arson. They are called "Arson Dogs." This means that they will be brought to a place where there has been a fire and will help to determine whether the fire was set deliberately or if it was an accident.

Children should NEVER play with fire.

Shown above is North Carolina State Bureau of Investigation Special Agent Andrew Bennett and K-9 Agent Aurora, a Labrador retriever/golden retriever who detects fire accelerants in fire/arson investigations.

K-9's Bene and Beny. Dep. D. Carter, S. Grantham, Sampson Count SD
Sampson County, NC

**Occasionally we fly in a helicopter
to get from place to place.
The chopper gives us a good view of the county and
takes us to our workplace rather quickly.
We call this chopper "Sable," and
it flies in North Carolina.**

But wherever we go, our handlers go with us.

K-9 Luka
Ofc. S. L. Lowery
Raleigh PD, Raleigh, NC

K-9 Nicki, 1985.
Ofc. Johnnie DeGeorgi
Landover Hill PD, L. H., MD

K-9 Jannsen
Ofc. R. Shirley
Haleyville PD,,Haleyville, AL

K-9 Loki (left) & Capt. James Kowalczk, K-9 Sam (center), Ofc. Paul Haraldson,
and K-9 Bullet (right) with Ofc. Todd Simonton.
All with the Bellevue Police Department, Bellevue, WA.

*Right: K-9 Chris & Ofc. D. Matson
Snellville PD, Snellville, GA*

*Left: Ofc. K. Vithalani and K-9 Arko
Wilmington PD*

We go to work with our "partner" every day, and sometimes work extra hours if the job demands it. Sometimes we wear a special vest that protects us, like K-9 Chris, in the picture above.

K-9 Nero, Ofc. K. A. Adams Raleigh Police Department, Raleigh, NC

K-9 Chris, Snellville PD, Snellville, GA

K-9 Clem and Ofc. Andrew Rebmann, Connecticut State Police. 1977. Clem was credited with over 200 trailing finds in his career.

Raleigh Police Department K-9 Unit. From left to right: Officers J. R. Mercer, K-9 Jens. R. L Warner, K-9 Onya. B. K. Stranahan, K-9 Marko. C. T. Barnett, K-9 Tuckey. P. T. Medlin, K-9 Otto. K-9 T. Pickens, K-9 Phantom. D. P. Green, K-9 Rudy. S. L. Lowery, K-9 Johnny. K. A. Adams, K-9 Kito. R. J. Hoyle, K-9 Jago. Raleigh, North Carolina.

K-9 Duke
Sampson County Sheriff Department
Sampson County, NC

K-9 Beny
Sampson County
Sheriff Dept.
Sampson County, NC

We are always rewarded for a job well done.

Sometimes our reward is a game of ball or a yummy treat.

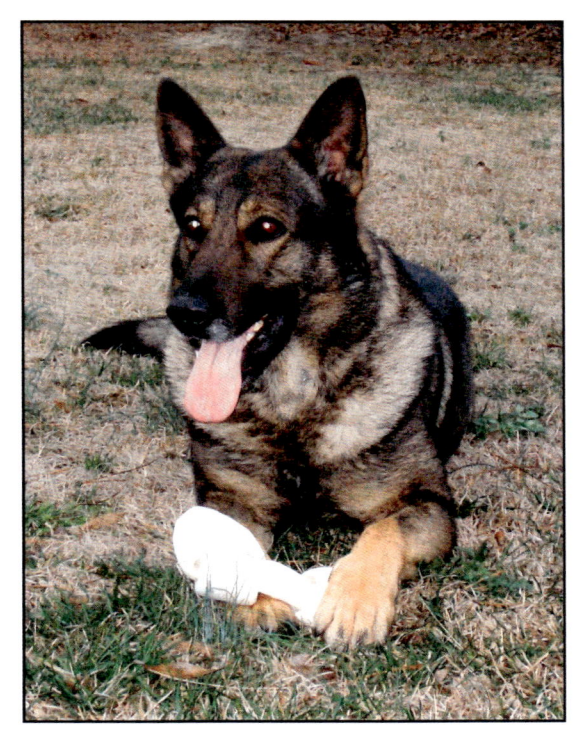

And at the end of the shift, we get to be just regular dogs.

On our days off we have fun with our handler. We are loved, just like other family pets.

K-9's Gola and Axe (on right)

*Ofc. P. T. Medllin,
Raleigh PD
Raleigh, NC*

*K-9 Otto
Raleigh PD
Raleigh, NC*

K-9 Loki, Bellevue Police Department, Bellevue, WA.   Charlie the Horse.

We might get to go swimming on a warm summer afternoon or decide to just relax at home.

*K-9 Ranger, Ready to Swim
Edmonds Police Department
Edmonds, WA*

*K-9 Loki, Undercover in his sunglasses.
Bellevue Police Department,
Bellevue, WA*

*K-9 Cyndi as Santa,
Wilmington PD,
Wilmington, NC*

Wilmington Police K-9 Division, Wilmington, NC

Our job….the K-9 Division.
Our duty: To protect and serve.

Our Prayer: To protect our handlers as they keep the community safe. They are *our* heroes.

The K-9 Cop

"A Prayer for Animals"

Hear our prayer ...
For all animals that are overworked, underfed and cruelly treated;
for any that are hunted, lost, deserted, frightened, or hungry;
and for those who deal with them, we ask a heart of compassion,
gentle hands, and kindly words."
~ Albert Schweitzer

K-9 Jago, Raleigh Police Department, Raleigh, NC

9-1-1 *We shall always remember.*

A Special Thanks

to all the departments, canine handlers, and canines who allowed us to use their photographs in this book. We appreciate all that you do to keep us safe.

Bellevue Police Department, Bellevue, WA
Officer: J. Kowalczyk   German Shepherd: K-9 Loki   Horse: Charlie - 27 years old

Brunswick County Sheriff Department, Brunswick County, NC
Deputies: Trainer Tommy Tolley, and J. Brown, B. Chism, J. Wall, B. Carlisle, J. Zeller, C. Sasser, D. Baldry, B. Simmons

K9's:	Bloodhounds:	K-9 Bonnie	K-9 Clyde
	German Shepherds:	K-9 Bruno	K-9 Carlos
	Belgian Malinois: K-9 Benny	K-9 Spike	K-9 Dicky
	K-9 Viper	K-9 Tax	K-9 Chico

DeKalb School Police Department, DeKalb County, GA
Officers: J. Brooks, J. R. Huff, T. Bell
K-9 Rocky, English Springer Spaniel   K-9 Tjibbe, Belgian Malinois
K-9 Tox, Belgian Malinois   K-9 Tax, Labrador Retriever

Edmonds Police Department, Edmonds, WA
Officers: P. Haraldson, T. Simonton, J. Kowalczyk
German Shepherds: K-9 Sam   K-9 Bullet   K-9 Ranger

Georgia State Bureau of Investigation Body Recovery Team and Floyd County Sheriff Department, GA
Officer T. Sargent   K-9 Cinco, German Shepherd

Haleyville Police Department, Haleyville, AL
Sgt. R. Shirley   K-9 Jannsen, Belgian Malinois

Iraq Special Contract Explosive Detection Dog
Handler: Jess Hunter   K-9 Zhirra, German Shepherd

Landover Hill Police Department, Landover Hill, Maryland
Officer J. DeGeorgi   K-9 Nicki, German Shepherd

New Hanover County Sheriff Department, New Hanover County, NC
    Deputy Charles G. Smith, Public Information Officer
    Handlers: C. Benton, S. Croom, J. Botbol, J. Stegall, C. Carey,
    R. Mills, W. Baxley
    K-9 Car, K-9 Bas, K-9 Fando, K-9 Sar, K-9 Motza, K-9 Bonnie, K-9 Nando

North Carolina State Bureau of Investigation, NC Department of Justice
    Attorney General Roy Cooper, PIO Officer Noelle Talley, and
    Handler - SBI Special Agent Andrew Bennett
    K-9: Agent Aurora, a Labrador Retriever/Golden Retriever

Raleigh Police Department, Raleigh, NC
    Officers: R. J. Hoyle, K. A. Adams, P. T. Medlin, C. T. Barnett, D. P. Green,
    S. L. Lowery, J. R. Mercer, R. L. Warner, B. K. Stranahan, K. T. Pickens,
    P.I. Kellogg
    German Shepherds:

K-9 Tuckey	K-9 Jens	K-9 Phantom	K-9 Marko
K-9 Onya	K-9 Otto	K-9 Axe	K-9 Chenok
K-9 Gola	K-9 Rocky	K-9 Behr	K-9 Reeko
K-9 Britt	K-9 Jago (from Solvakia)		

    Belgian Malinois:

K-9 Luka	K-9 Rudy	K-9 Kito
	K-9 Nero (from Holland)	K-9 Elsie

Sampson County Sheriff Department, Sampson County, NC
    Deputies: S. Grantham and D. Carter
    German Shepherds: K-9 Beny, imported from the Czech Republic
                                K-9 Bene, imported from Holland
                                K-9 Rex, Retired in 2008
    Bloodhound: K-9 Duke, born in the USA

Snellville Police Department, Snellville, Georgia
    Officer D. R. Matson   Belgian Malinois, K-9 Chris

Wilmington Police Department, Wilmington, North Carolina
    Officers: Kirti J. Vithalani, T. Poelling, D. Pellegrino, C. Seitter,
    S. Brister, C. Stansbury
    German Shepherds: K-9 Arko   K-9 Huck
    Belgian Malinois: K-9 Rudy K-9 Deon K-9 Igor K-9 Bronco K-9 Cyndi
    Dutch Shepherd: K-9 Bruno

Printed in the United States of America.

Made in the USA
Las Vegas, NV
14 July 2022